BURLINGTON NORTHERN
THE FINAL YEARS

Mike Danneman

AMBERLEY

First published 2022

Amberley Publishing
The Hill, Stroud
Gloucestershire, GL5 4EP

www.amberley-books.com

The right of Mike Danneman to be identified
as the Author of this work has been asserted in
accordance with the Copyrights, Designs and
Patents Act 1988.

ISBN 978 1 3981 0315 3 (print)
ISBN 978 1 3981 0316 0 (ebook)

British Library Cataloguing in Publication Data.
A catalogue record for this book is available from
the British Library.

Typesetting by SJmagic DESIGN SERVICES, India.
Printed in the UK.

Introduction

Burlington Northern was created on 2 March 1970. Serving nineteen states and two Canadian provinces, it became the largest railroad in the United States. The merger of the Chicago, Burlington & Quincy Railroad, Great Northern Railway, Northern Pacific Railway and Spokane, Portland & Seattle Railway fashioned a colossal 25,000-mile railroad.

In its infancy, BN still operated and maintained a large quantity of vintage power obtained from its predecessor railroads. A growing traffic base and booming Powder River Basin coal tonnage in Wyoming demanded massive quantities of additional locomotives and coal-hauling cars. More than 1,500 new locomotives were added to the roster in the 1970s. Each one of these modern and reliable higher-horsepower units allowed BN to retire many older locomotives in the 1980s. All locomotives were painted a unified Cascade green and black, ending a 'rainbow' look to the fleet when the last engine was cloaked in green on 9 September 1977. But this didn't last long, as BN looked to expand its territory.

The 21 November 1980 merger of St. Louis–San Francisco Railway, better known as the Frisco, brought BN into the flourishing Southeast and added more diverse traffic in five additional states. With an expanded system, new Portland to Birmingham freight began service. Operating over 3,000 miles at the time, it was the longest through freight operation on a single railroad. Frisco's flag disappeared fairly quickly, as all its locomotives were painted in BN colors or retired by 31 July 1983.

The Staggers Act, signed on 14 October 1980, deregulated most freight transportation in the U.S., creating more competition, and on the BN this freedom brought a new emphasis on pricing and service. BN began 'Expediter' intermodal trains on its former Frisco lines in 1985, the same year the first double-stack container train began operating. Expediters used two-man crews, took new business off the highways and soon expanded to other parts of the system. To capture more domestic intermodal business, the railroad established BN America in 1989, a service offering door-to-door domestic container service. From 1980 to 1990, BN more than doubled its intermodal volume.

Burlington Northern was at one time the twelfth largest owner of forest land in the U.S., dating back to land grants given to NP as incentive for its construction, so lumber products have always been a part of BN's traffic mix. The railroad was also the one of nation's largest grain carriers, hauling 447,000 carloads in 1990. But the big story on BN in the 1980s continued to be the explosive growth of coal shipments from Powder River Basin. Over the years, the coal business required huge amounts of capital investments in track construction, locomotives, cars and upgrading many existing routes to handle the tonnage. Coal was 33 per cent of BN's revenue in 1991. That year, nearly 9 per cent of all electricity generated in the U.S. was produced from coal hauled by BN.

Developed by the New York industrial design firm of Lippincott & Margulies, BN's Cascade green and black, with diagonal white nose stripes, scheme for locomotives remained a constant for much of its history. But by 1985, BN was looking to increase visibility of its trains and experimented with adding orange and black to the nose. A group of units arrived on the property that year, including fifty-three new EMD GP50s painted in the 'tiger-stripe' scheme.

Even more radical than a new paint scheme, 'power-by-the-hour' was developed for locomotives by BN and introduced in 1986. Under the arrangement, outside owners purchase new locomotives for BN, with the railroad buying only the electrical power generated by the locomotives. A hundred EMD SD60 Oakway locomotives arrived in 1986, with 100 GE B39-8 LMX locomotives joining the roster in 1987/8. Even though the power-by-the-hour concept was a success, complicated legal and financial agreements caused BN to revert to conventional locomotive purchases again, beginning with the EMD SD60M model.

Still wanting to improve visibility of its units, BN chose a revised rendition of its standard Cascade green, white and black colors in April 1989. The new livery featured a white cab front, with nose stripes replaced with a large white BN herald on a green background, and was quickly dubbed the 'whiteface' scheme. Beginning in 1988, BN had large groups of older locomotives remanufactured, adding an additional twenty-year lifespan to a rebuilt locomotive. Most were painted in the new 'whiteface' scheme.

Following four BN EMD SD60MAC testbed locomotives built in 1992, BN entered the AC revolution in a big way when it placed a $675 million order for 350 EMD SD70MAC locomotives in 1993. At this time all freight locomotives in the U. S. relied on DC (direct current) traction motors on their locomotives. Simply put, AC (alternating current) traction motors are simpler, more reliable, more efficient and more durable than regular DC traction motors. The electrical system of an AC locomotive is more complex and expensive, but as a cost-saving measure BN was able to take five DC traction locomotives used on coal trains and replace them with three new EMD SD70MAC locomotives.

These innovative locomotives also introduced BN's final paint scheme. The European-inspired paint scheme that first appeared on BN's pair of Executive F units and business trains was also applied to the new SD70MACs. The main color was a deep forest green, latter dubbed 'Grinstein green' for BN president and CEO, Gerald Grinstein, the man behind the new colors. This dark green is tastefully highlighted with a wide band of creme color, which also envelopes the cab, and is accented with twin red pinstripes.

By the mid-1980s, when coverage of the Burlington Northern in this book begins, it was clearly a unique and established railroad, not just a colorful collection of its five merger partners. Through years of changes and growth, BN entered the final decade of its life stronger than ever. It survived deregulation, downsizing, and the usual corporate restructuring to become one of America's premier railroads. The final years saw the railroad continue to grow, following a path to the Santa Fe combination, forming powerhouse BNSF as a capstone to its short life.

Photos of Burlington Northern featured in this book are arranged chronologically from 1983 to 1996, and all were captured by the author. BN and Santa Fe became BNSF through a holding company on 22 September 1995, and their operating departments were formally merged on 31 December 1996, when BN officially disappeared into the history books. I didn't venture to every corner of the sprawling BN system, but I hope you enjoy some views of the places I did visit during the final years of the Burlington Northern Railroad.

BURLINGTON NORTHERN—1992

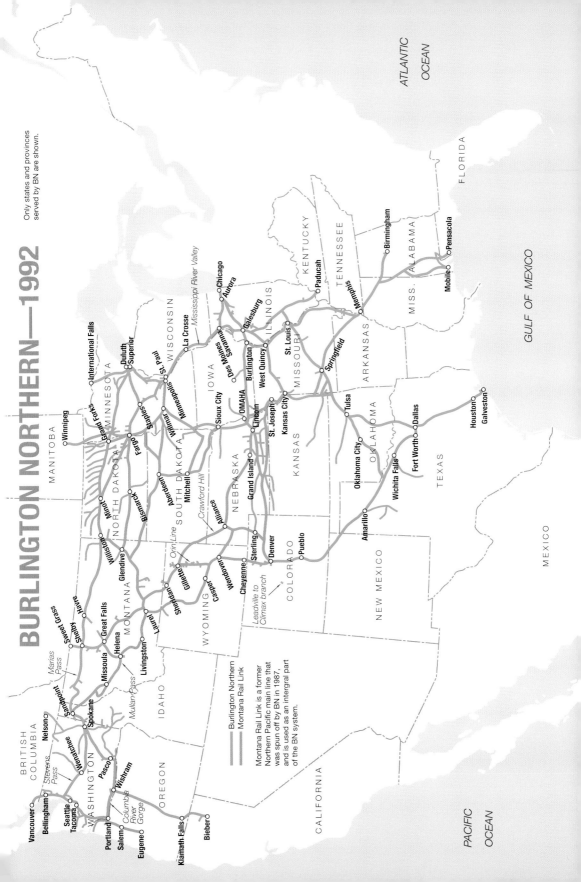

Only states and provinces served by BN are shown.

| Burlington Northern |
| Montana Rail Link |

Montana Rail Link is a former Northern Pacific main line that was spun off by BN in 1987, and is used as an integral part of the BN system.

ATLANTIC OCEAN

PACIFIC OCEAN

GULF OF MEXICO

MEXICO

Provinces/States:
BRITISH COLUMBIA, MANITOBA, WASHINGTON, OREGON, IDAHO, MONTANA, NORTH DAKOTA, SOUTH DAKOTA, MINNESOTA, WISCONSIN, WYOMING, NEBRASKA, IOWA, ILLINOIS, COLORADO, KANSAS, MISSOURI, KENTUCKY, TENNESSEE, OKLAHOMA, ARKANSAS, MISS., ALABAMA, FLORIDA, NEW MEXICO, TEXAS, CALIFORNIA

Cities and features:
Vancouver, Bellingham, Seattle, Tacoma, Portland, Salem, Eugene, Klamath Falls, Bieber, Wishram, Pasco, Wenatchee, Nelson, Sandpoint, Spokane, Missoula, Helena, Great Falls, Shelby, Sweet Grass, Havre, Livingston, Laurel, Minot, Williston, Glendive, Bismarck, Sheridan, Casper, Wendover, Cheyenne, Sterling, Denver, Pueblo, Alliance, Aberdeen, Mitchell, Grand Island, Winnipeg, Grand Forks, Fargo, Staples, Willmar, Minneapolis, St. Paul, Duluth, Superior, International Falls, La Crosse, Sioux City, OMAHA, Lincoln, St. Joseph, Kansas City, Des Moines, Savanna, Burlington, West Quincy, Galesburg, Aurora, Chicago, St. Louis, Springfield, Tulsa, Oklahoma City, Wichita Falls, Fort Worth, Dallas, Amarillo, Houston, Galveston, Paducah, Memphis, Birmingham, Mobile, Pensacola

Marias Pass, Stevens Pass, Mullan Pass, Columbia River Gorge, Mississippi River Valley, Orin Line, Crawford Hill, Leadville to Climax branch

For many years after the formation of Chicago's commuter agency, Metra, Burlington Northern still leased and operated a fleet of twenty-five vintage, rebuilt EMD E8A and E9A cab units. A commuter train heads west after a quick stop at Stone Avenue at La Grange, Illinois, in August 1983, led by venerable E unit No. 9904.

Burlington Northern's 23rd Street diesel shop in Denver, Colorado, is a sea of Cascade green in April 1984. A good assortment of EMD and GE locomotives dressed in the uniformity of the original paint scheme are identifiable, including five SD9s, three SD40-2s, three B30-7As, two U30Cs, and one each of F45, GP30, GP20 models.

Rolling past farm fields sprouting spring plants, a BN local passes the approach signal for the crossing of Chicago & North Western's Peoria line between Rock Falls and Harmon, Illinois, on 10 June 1984. BN operated this former Chicago, Burlington & Quincy branch from Sterling to Earlville, and by this date, trackage of the branch was deteriorating. With traffic dwindling, trains would soon not be running on this 46.8-mile-long line, and it would be torn up in 1985.

Just after putting a two-car train away in the yard and spotting caboose No. 10286, the crew of EMD SD9 No. 6223 has put the locomotive to rest inside the spiffy-looking wooden roundhouse at Leadville, Colorado, in July 1984. The train just made a trip to the molybdenum mine at Climax, at an elevation of 11,400 feet, making this run the highest standard gauge rail operation in the U.S. at the time. Burlington Northern predecessor Colorado & Southern had an extensive narrow gauge network in the mountains of Colorado, but by 1941 only this 14-mile branch from Leadville to Climax remained. The line was isolated from the rest of the system, and a rail connection to the outside world existed through Rio Grande's Leadville Branch and Tennessee Pass route to Pueblo.

Yes, there really was a Cascade green Burlington Northern locomotive numbered 1. BN had a former Great Northern NW2 constructed in 1939 on the roster, rebuilt it into a NW2R in 1975 and renumbered No. 1. In September 1984, the spiffy-looking switcher was located at Minneapolis Junction, Minnesota.

Burlington Northern SW1000 switchers Nos 394 and 393 haul a transfer freight through West Hoffman past Dayton's Bluff in St Paul, Minnesota, in September 1984. Both locomotives were built by EMD in October 1972.

Heavy with loaded vehicles up front, a BN freight curves toward the Wisconsin State Highway 16 overpass after departing the crew change point of La Crosse in September 1984. Former Frisco EMD SD40-2 No. 6845 leads a pair of EMD SD45s as power on the eastbound train.

Burlington Northern EMD SD9 No. 6102 switches a cut of cars at the railroad's Northtown Yard in September 1984. Looming above the locomotive in the background is the city of Minneapolis, Minnesota.

Burlington Northern EMD GP9 No. 1916 leads a fourteen-car local freight around the wye at M&D Junction, heading for a trip south on the former Northern Pacific 'Skally Line' at White Bear Lake, Minnesota, in September 1984. This is home territory for the 1916, as it is the former NP No. 331, built in 1957.

Splattered with shiny black oil, a Burlington Northern EMD SD40-2 with a blown turbocharger waits for repair at the railroad's Burlington Shops at West Burlington, Iowa, on 27 January 1985.

It's an all-EMD BN line up at the small locomotive facility at Sterling, Colorado, on 7 July 1985. Left to right are SD40-2 No. 7801, GP20 No. 2059 and SD9 No. 6172.

A Burlington Northern coal empty approaches the top of the grade at Palmer Lake on Colorado's Joint Line on the afternoon of 8 July 1985. Four GE C30-7s lead a lone EMD SD40-2 as power for the train that is headed for Denver and eventual loading at a mine in Wyoming's Powder River Basin.

Snaking along the edge of the North Platte River through Wendover Canyon is a Burlington Northern coal train between Wendover and Cassa, Wyoming, on 18 July 1985. Five locomotives, elephant-style, power the train – an EMD SD40-2 is followed by three GE C30-7s and a GE U30C.

BN coal trains meet at Cairo, Nebraska, on the railroad's busy conduit for coal tonnage, the Ravenna Subdivision, on the afternoon of 19 July 1985. Cairo is a small town located between the crew change at Ravenna and Grand Island.

Burlington Northern U30C No. 5908 leads an eastbound coal train at Broken Bow, Nebraska, on 19 July 1985. Hauling coal as it was built to do, No. 5908 was constructed by General Electric in December 1972.

A pair of EMD SD9s rumble eastward through Brookston, Minnesota, with a Burlington Northern local freight on 19 October 1985. The train is about to pass under U.S. Highway 2 overpass just east of Brookston siding.

A westbound Burlington Northern local freight – comprised of two EMD GP20s, six wood chip gons and a caboose – zips past the wood frame station at Cromwell, Minnesota, on 19 October 1985.

Cabooses on the end of two BN trains pass MJ Tower on the south side of Superior, Wisconsin, on 20 October 1985. Waiting for BN traffic to clear is Missabe's Steelton Switch with three EMD SD9s, which is returning from interchanging cars with the Soo Line at their Stinson Yard. Why the southbound train has three cabooses is unknown, but for now at least, cabooses still reigned on the rear of trains on the route to and from the twin ports of Duluth and Superior.

A Burlington Northern double-stack train passes Hoffman Avenue at Dayton's Bluff in St Paul, Minnesota, on 22 March 1986. A pair of EMD GP50s in the tiger-stripe paint scheme bracket a GE B30-7A 'B-unit' as A-B-A power for the westbound train.

In the mid-1980s, BN was operating two to three trains from 31st Street Yard in Denver out to the Coors Brewery in Golden, Colorado, on a daily basis. For a good portion of this time, there was a trio of former Great Northern EMD SDP40s powering the train. On 14 July 1986, BN Nos 6398, 6395 and 6397 get underway eastbound out of Golden after picking up its train at the Coors interchange.

A BN freight thunders westbound on Track 2 through Highlands, Illinois, on 2 August 1986. The train is led by BN No. 6593 – former Great Northern EMD SDP45 No. 327 – one of eight originally equipped with a steam generator for passenger service when purchased by GN in 1967.

Burlington Northern EMD locomotives gather at the locomotive facility at Clyde Yard in Cicero, Illinois. BN F45 No. 6642 is flanked by GP9 No. 1877 and GP50 No. 3141 on the whisker tracks off the turntable near the old roundhouse on 23 November 1986.

A quartet of Burlington Northern EMD GP50s in tiger-stripe paint, spliced by a fuel tender, wheel a westbound intermodal train out of Chicago at La Grange, Illinois, on 7 February 1987. My notes don't say, but this is either train 3 or 13, beginning its long trip to the west coast.

A westbound BN intermodal train flies through Highlands, Illinois, on 18 April 1987. Leading the train is EMD GP50 Nos 3107 and 3118, followed by a fuel tender, a GE B30-7A 'B unit' and another GP50. BN 3107 was ordered by the Frisco, but was delivered after the merger painted in Cascade green of BN.

Burlington Northern train 3 slips through a cut west of Oregon, Illinois, on 22 August 1987. Powered by two EMD GP50s dressed in tiger stripes, splicing a fuel tender and a GE B30-7A B unit, today's train has a cut of auto racks up front.

General Electric U30C No. 5828 leads an eastbound Burlington Northern coal train at Hoffman Avenue below Dayton's Bluff at St Paul, Minnesota, on a sunny 21 November 1987.

A BN intermodal train rolls through the St Croix interlocking with Milwaukee Road near Hastings, Minnesota, on 21 November 1987. BN EMD SD40-2 No. 7099, built in November 1978, leads the Chicago-bound train.

Waiting at an approach signal for single track at Palmer Lake at a location known as the 'Sag' near Spruce is a southbound Burlington Northern coal train. Four new Oakway Leasing EMD SD60s, along with a EMD BN SD40-2 and a GE U30C power the train on Colorado's Joint Line on 14 July 1987.

A pair of Burlington Northern GE C30-7s bracket a pair of Oakway Leasing EMD SD60s leading a coal train that is grinding up the grade through Larkspur on 24 February 1988. The train is crossing the bridge over Spruce Mountain Road, with this portion of the southbound main located here owned by the Santa Fe on Colorado's Joint Line between Denver and Pueblo.

With two blue and white Oakway Leasing EMD SD60s leading, a southbound BN coal train curves through Palmer Lake, Colorado, on 24 February 1988.

Beneath the spectacular mountains of Glacier National Park, an eastbound Burlington Northern grain train crosses Two Medicine Bridge at East Glacier, Montana, on 3 March 1988. A trio of EMD SD40-2s bracketing a lone GE B30-7A provides the necessary locomotion.

On 3 March 1988, a westbound Burlington Northern train faces a strong snowstorm at Summit, Montana, on Marias Pass. Between BN EMD No. 7164 and another sister locomotive is a Rio Grande EMD SD40T-2 Tunnel Motor, surely accustomed to winter snow and high altitudes.

A trio of Burlington Northern EMD SD40-2s pull a westbound intermodal train downgrade on the west slope of Marias Pass east of Java, Montana, on a snowy 3 March 1988.

Atop Marias Pass on a snowy 3 March 1988, tiger-striped Burlington Northern EMD GP50 No. 3152 leads an eastbound freight through a blizzard at Summit, Montana. Trailing No. 3152 are two more GP50s, a GE B30-7A and two EMD SD40-2s.

Still hauling passengers as Electro-Motive Division intended, a trio of Burlington Northern E9A locomotives line up with commuter trains in the BN/Metra Hill Yard at Aurora, Illinois, on 16 April 1988. At this time, they were as common as a SD40-2-powered freight train on BN's triple-track main line out of Chicago – but nothing lasts forever.

Burlington Northern train 203 gets passed by a BN commuter train at Eola, Illinois, on the afternoon of 11 June 1988. Leading the freight is EMD GP40-2 No. 3055, while the commuter train is led by venerable EMD E9A No. 9925.

Three BN GE C30-7s smoke it up as they depart Tamora, Nebraska, on the morning of 2 July 1988. The train held the main for a meet and is now bringing the coal loads back into motion, while another eastbound coal train waits right behind.

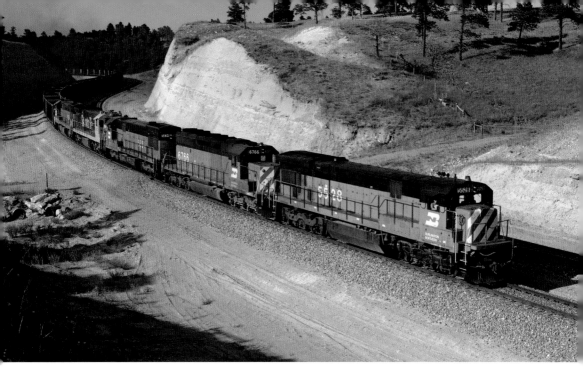

A BN coal train slugs it out on the grade of Nebraska's Crawford Hill as the train approaches the top at Belmont on 3 July 1988. Powering the train is GE C30-7 No. 5528, EMD SD40-2 No. 6766, GE U30C No. 5834, Santa Fe GE C30-7 No. 8117 and another BN GE U30C.

Burlington Northern and Kansas City Southern locomotives power a westbound BN coal train departing Guernsey, Wyoming, on the Canyon Subdivision on 4 July 1988. The empty train is headed back to Powder River Basin for loading and is crossing the North Platte River in the background.

BN train 2 is tucked in the siding at Carter, Illinois, to meet BN train 203, powered by a pair of Cascade green EMD SD40-2s, on 15 October 1988. The engineer on No. 2 waves from the cab of LMX No. 8500 as another crew member is on the ground on the opposite side of the main for a visual inspection of both sides of the westbound freight.

Burlington Northern train 203 cruises through Stratford, Illinois, on 15 October 1988. The westbound freight is powered by two members of BN's huge EMD SD40-2 fleet.

On 1 March 1989, a quartet of Oakway Leasing EMD SD60s power a Burlington Northern grain train over Montana's Marias Pass. Marching westbound through Marias in a lightly falling snow on this frigid day are Oakway Nos 9011, 9009, 9046 and 9094.

A BN freight heads across Java Bridge at Java, Montana, on a frigid 2 March 1989. Trailing lead tiger-striped EMD GP50 No. 3126 is a SD40-2, another GP50, a GE B30-7A and a fuel tender.

With a fresh crew aboard, an eastbound Burlington Northern freight is about to depart Whitefish, Montana, amid a light snowfall on 2 March 1989.

Two sets of Burlington Northern SD40-2 helpers rest in front of the Izaak Walton Inn at Essex, Montana, on a cold 2 March 1989. Soon enough, another call to push a train up Marias Pass will be answered by these trusty locomotives. The inn was built by Great Northern in 1939, and today still caters to travelers visiting Glacier National Park and exploring Montana's wilderness.

Raising is own rooster tail of blowing snow is an eastbound BN freight at Grizzly, Montana, beneath the towering peaks of Glacier National Park on 3 March 1989. The train is led by BN No. 3501, a former CB&Q GP40 that was remanufactured by Morrison-Knudsen in 1988.

A BN grain train passes through a frigid Bison, Montana, while negotiating a winter crossing of Marias Pass on 3 March 1989. Four EMD SD40-2s and a lone GE B30-7A power the westbound train.

Three Burlington Northern helper sets, made up of pairs of EMD SD40-2 locomotives, are stationed at Essex, Montana, to help heavy trains over 5,213-foot-high Marias Pass on 4 March 1989.

A BN commuter train, also known locally as a 'dinky', ducks under the signal bridge at Naperville, Illinois, on the afternoon of 15 April 1989. We are 26.2 miles west of Chicago Union Station on BN's busy triple-track main line.

Passing under the wooden overpass of South Burlington Road, Burlington Northern train 13 curves through a cut west of Oregon, Illinois, on 1 April 1989. Hustling the intermodal train destined for Portland, Oregon, is BN EMD GP50 No. 3114, in original tiger-stripe paint, and GE B30-7A B unit No. 4116.

BN GE C30-7 No. 5017 leads an eastbound coal train out of Tamora, Nebraska, on the bright morning of 1 July 1989. Spending most of their lives hauling coal as intended, BN amassed 242 GE C30-7s on its locomotive roster between 1976 and 1981.

Slowly climbing over Pine Ridge, a BN coal train works upgrade on Crawford Hill between Crawford and Belmont, Nebraska, on the afternoon of 2 July 1989.

A Burlington Northern coal train grinds up Crawford Hill, west of Belmont, Nebraska, on 2 July 1989. The train is powered by two BN GE C30-7s and three EMD SD40-2s (BN 7239, along with Kansas City Southern Nos 691 and 666) and is pushed on the rear by three more BN SD40-2s splicing a fuel tender, which are just disappearing behind the hillside on the track below in the background.

The helper locomotives in the previous photo are now shown shoving hard on the rear of the coal train as they curve past Breezy Point west of Belmont on Nebraska's Crawford Hill on 2 July 1989. The fuel tender used in the set provides more time between refueling stops.

Two Burlington Northern trains meet on Crawford Hill, Nebraska, at Breezy Point (also sometimes known as Windy Point) on a hot 3 July 1989. The westbound grain train is rolling downgrade on Track 1 as a heavy coal train pounds away eastbound on Track 2. Up front is 2 EMD SD40-2s, 2 GE C30-7s and a GE U30C, while shoving hard on the rear on the other side of the big horseshoe curve are three more SD40-2s splicing a fuel tender.

An eastbound Burlington Northern intermodal train meets a westbound coal empty at Orella, Nebraska, on 3 July 1989. Leading the intermodal is LMX GE B39-8 No. 8558. BN operated a fleet of 100 of these locomotives from LMX, paying for kilowatt/hours generated in freight service to the lessor.

BN's Crawford local rolls over the top of Crawford Hill at Belmont, Nebraska, on the morning of 3 July 1989, with cars for interchange to the Chicago & North Western at Crawford.

An eastbound Burlington Northern coal train snakes out of Newcastle, Wyoming, on 3 July 1989. Powering the train are EMD SD40-2 No. 7266, GE U30C No. 5389, GE C30-7 No. 5023, EMD SD40-2 No. 7120 and GE C30-7 No. 5509.

On 4 July 1989, a northbound Burlington Northern coal train passes by the siding at Walker, Wyoming, as it heads for a Powder River Basin coal mine on the Orin Line. The 127.3-mile-long Orin Line was built in the late 1970s to access the flourishing coal mines located in Powder River Basin.

A Burlington Northern freight, powered by a pair of GE B39-8s, heads south through Sedalia, Colorado, on the morning of 7 July 1989. Colorado's Joint Line was shared trackage between South Denver and Brandon (Pueblo) by Rio Grande and Santa Fe, with Burlington Northern (Colorado & Southern) trains also having the same operating rights on the route.

Burlington Northern intermodal train 13 passes BN freight train 103 at Burke, Illinois, on 7 April 1990. The two trains just swapped crews so the slower and delayed train 103, with EMD GP39M No. 2830, can still make the next crew change point of La Crosse, Wisconsin.

BN train 103 cruises along the Mississippi River just west of Savanna, Illinois, on the afternoon of 7 April 1990. BN GP39M No. 2830 is former Chicago, Burlington & Quincy EMD GP30 No. 944, built in April 1962 and rebuilt by Morrison-Knudsen in October 1989.

On 13 July 1990, a westbound Burlington Northern coal train traverses the Brush Subdivision between Hillrose and Brush, Colorado. From Brush, the train will travel to Denver and head south to a power plant in Texas.

Burlington Northern train 42, an 'Expediter' intermodal train, cruises along the Mississippi River just north (west) of Savanna, Illinois, on 13 October 1990.

BN EMD GP39M No. 2805 leads westbound 'Expediter' train 41 out of Savanna, Illinois, on the afternoon of 13 October 1990. The first few rebuilds of GP30s into GP39Ms by Morrison-Knudsen in 1988 were painted in the then-current original BN striped-nose scheme, like No. 2805.

Burlington Northern EMD GP50 Nos 3112 and 3151, along with a GP39M (rebuilt GP30), rest at the Clyde Yard locomotive facility at Cicero, Illinois, on 26 January 1991.

Passing a yard switcher taking a short break, Burlington Northern train 154 enters Galesburg Yard on 17 February 1991. The sprawling yard at Galesburg is a major facility for BN and is located south-west of Chicago in central Illinois.

Burlington Northern 'Expediter' intermodal train 41 is about to clatter across the Chicago Central diamonds at East Dubuque, Illinois, on 10 March 1991. This very unique track arrangement is at the west end of shared trackage (Burlington/Illinois Central – later BN/CC) where the CC main line curves away from the BN's line near the East Dubuque depot, enters a curved tunnel through a bluff, pops out of the bore and immediately crosses the BN double-track main line, and onto a bridge over the Mississippi River. A model railroad-like track arrangement and scene!

A short Burlington Northern local out of Rochelle, Illinois, scurries westward on the C&I (Chicago & Iowa, a predecessor) line west of Flag Center on 6 April, 1991. Between EMD GP38 No. 2172 and caboose No. 11773 is a lone Chicago & North Western boxcar.

Crossing the Rock River Bridge at Oregon, Illinois, is Burlington Northern train 103 on the nice spring day of 6 April 1991. On this particular day, the train was restricted to 35 mph, making for a nice chase, and we followed 103 the rest of the afternoon until the last photo at Savanna during sunset.

BN train 4 curves out of Rochelle, Illinois, on the morning of 6 April 1991. The locomotive still looks like a GP30 as EMD intended when built in February 1963, only it was originally built as Cotton Belt No. 5007, and rebuilt by Morrison-Knudsen into BN GP39M No. 2803.

Burlington Northern train 43 growls out of the siding at Chana, Illinois, after meeting train 2 on the sunny spring day of 6 April 1991. On the point is GP20C No. 2003, a rebuilt EMD GP20 repowered with a Caterpillar engine. Trailing is sister Cat No. 2008 and an EMD GP39M.

An overview of BN's 23rd Street locomotive facility in Denver, Colorado, on 18 May 1991, reveals some interesting sights. Up front are locomotives used on BN's 'beer run' trains from Denver out to Coors Brewing in Golden – a trio of EMD SDP40s – Nos 6398, 6397 and 6399. Ten EMD SD9s are gathered, along with a trio of Santa Fe EMD SD40-2s. On the left is a group of GE B39-8 LMX units, mixed into some Cascade green SD40-2s. In the middle of it all is an upside-down BN ballast hopper No. 95834, its predicament unusual and unknown.

An eastbound Burlington Northern freight has followed the Mississippi River since departing St Paul, Minnesota, and is now approaching Savanna, Illinois, on 20 July 1991. Just outside of town, the tracks will divide, with one route headed toward Galesburg and the other veering away from 'Old Man River' and across a rolling farmland to Chicago.

On 8 August 1991, an eastbound Burlington Northern coal train, led by new EMD SD60M No. 9297, passes the old grain elevators at Taylor, North Dakota.

A BN coal train passes through a wide, deep cut located just east of the Missouri River Bridge between the crew change of Mandan and Bismarck, North Dakota, on the afternoon of 8 August 1991.

A Burlington Northern coal train curves its way east past milepost 143 just west of Sully Springs, North Dakota, on 9 August 1991. Two EMD SD60Ms and two EMD SD40-2s power the train through the rugged Badlands.

After meeting an eastbound BN coal load at Sully Springs, North Dakota, a westbound train departs the siding on the afternoon of 9 August 1991. The empties are powered by three fresh Cascade green EMD SD60Ms and a lone EMD SD40-2.

Traversing the scenic Badlands, a Burlington Northern coal train grinds through the 's' curve at milepost 143 just west of Sully Springs, North Dakota, on the morning of 10 August 1991. Three new EMD SD60Ms pair up with an older EMD SD40-2 on this eastbound train.

An eastbound Burlington Northern coal train changes crews in front of the depot at Dickinson, North Dakota, on the morning of 10 August 1991.

Just moments after departing the crew change town of Mandan, North Dakota, on the afternoon of 10 August 1991, a westbound BN coal train crosses a truss bridge over the Heart River.

A late afternoon sun gets low to the horizon and lights up a westbound Burlington Northern coal train sweeping through a curve west of Lyons, North Dakota, on 10 August 1991.

In Valley City, North Dakota, a westbound BN coal train crosses the massive High Bridge over the Sheyenne River on 11 August 1991. Built between 1906 and 1908, the 3,860-foot-long bridge soars 162 feet above the river.

Burlington Northern GP9 No. 1858 and Fort Worth & Denver caboose No. 185 are assigned to local service at Mendota, Illinois, and wait for their next call of duty on the night of 24 August 1991. BN No. 1848 was built in 1955 as Northern Pacific No. 232.

Burlington Northern train 2 speeds eastbound (southward at this location) out of Genoa, Wisconsin, on 12 October 1991. The lead locomotive is former Great Northern GP35 No. 3021, rebuilt by EMD in 1989 and becoming BN GP39E No. 2933.

An eastbound Burlington Northern intermodal train rolls through Victory, Wisconsin, late in the afternoon of 12 October 1991. Behind EMD GP50 No. 3127 and GP40M No. 3511 is business car 'Columbia River'.

Burlington Northern train 34 heads over Two Medicine Bridge at East Glacier, Montana, on 29 February 1992. The eastbound vehicle train is powered by EMD SD40-2 Nos 6384 and 8165 spliced by EMD SD40 No. 6323.

BN intermodal train 1, powered by a pair of GE B39-8 LMX locomotives, approaches Shed 10 as it descends Marias Pass between Blacktail and Nimrod, Montana, on the afternoon of 29 February 1992.

Geraniums are neatly planted along the platform at Hinsdale, Illinois, making the pleasant spring afternoon feel even more like summer on 28 May 1992. BN's busy triple-track main line is seeing the afternoon rush of commuter trains pass through, as a westbound BN 'dinky' accelerates after discharging passengers at the station stop of Hinsdale.

On the beautiful spring morning of 7 June 1992, an eastbound Burlington Northern intermodal train, led by a pair of EMD GP50s, crosses the Wisconsin River at Crawford, east of Prairie du Chien, Wisconsin.

A loaded BN coal train holds down the siding at Berea, Nebraska, on the morning of 24 July 1992. Lead locomotive GE C30-7 No. 5057 has been repainted in BN's 'whiteface' paint scheme.

An eastbound BN coal train is entering the horseshoe curve below Belmont while climbing Nebraska's Crawford Hill on the morning of 24 July 1992.

A helper locomotive set comprised of a quartet of EMD SD40-2 splicing a fuel tender push hard on a heavy coal train climbing through the large horseshoe curve below Belmont, Nebraska, on 24 July 1992.

Aiming its nose into a lowering sun is BN EMD SD60M No. 9226 leading a westbound coal train through Terry, Montana, on 26 July 1992.

Three Burlington Northern EMD SD60Ms power an eastbound coal train through the Badlands past milepost 145, east of Medora, North Dakota, on 27 July 1992.

In 1990, BN converted EMD SD40-2 No. 7890 to burn natural gas fuel as an experiment to lower fuel costs and get cleaner exhaust emissions. The work was performed at Coast Engine & Equipment (CEECO) in Tacoma, Washington. The job included SD45-like flared radiators due to the need for increased cooling capacities to go with the hotter operating temperatures the unit endures while burning natural gas. It also received modified power assemblies, including new pistons, and a special paint job. In the morning sun on 27 July 1992, No. 7890 sits at the engine facility at Glendive, Montana.

Burlington Northern train 2 glides along the banks of the Mississippi River just west (north) of Savanna, Illinois, on a sunny 25 October 1992. The Chicago-bound intermodal train is powered by a pair of EMD GP50s.

Lone GE LMX B39-8 8521 pulls 'Expediter' intermodal train 41 around a curve just east of Burke, Illinois, late in the day of 25 October 1992.

Powered by a pair of EMD SD40-2s, an eastbound BN intermodal train follows a frozen Mississippi River into Savanna, Illinois, on the afternoon of 30 January 1993.

BN train 144 crosses one of the truss bridges over the Sinsinawa River west of Portage, Illinois, on the morning of 5 June 1993. Lead locomotive No. 7301 is a former Missouri Pacific SD40 that was reconditioned by Morrison-Knudsen for GATX and leased to BN.

Burlington Northern's Helena turn crosses Bridge 182.7 in Wolf Creek Canyon west of Wolf Creek, Montana, on 25 August 1993. The train is powered by EMD GP39M No. 2885 and EMD SD40 No. 6304, and is operating on the 95.4-mile former Great Northern line from Great Falls to Helena.

On 25 August 1993, Burlington Northern's Helena turn trundles through Silver City, Montana, on its trip to Helena. The large station signs were unique to BN.

Equipped with A.C. traction motors and radial trucks, Burlington Northern's pioneering EMD SD60MACs were tested by other railroads interested in the new technology. On 17 October 1993, Soo Line was testing BN's SD60MACs, Nos 9500, 9503 and 9502, on Soo Line train 430 heading up 2nd Street in downtown Bellevue, Iowa.

The trees are verdant green along the rocky bluffs lining the Mississippi River at Cassville, Wisconsin, as an eastbound Burlington Northern intermodal train cuts a straight path through the scene in a view from Nelson Dewey State Park on the morning of 28 May 1994.

A westbound BN vehicle train passes the entrance to the Stonefield Historic Site at Cassville, Wisconsin, on 28 May 1994. Stonefield is the 2,000-acre estate of Wisconsin's first governor, Nelson Dewey, that features more than thirty buildings in a beautiful setting that celebrates Wisconsin's rich agricultural heritage for all to enjoy.

Two Burlington Northern EMD SD60Ms lead a coal train over the Missouri River Bridge at Bismarck, North Dakota, on the morning of 29 June 1994. This big bridge links the crew change and servicing point of Mandan with the state capital on this scenic former Northern Pacific main line.

A BN freight heads west through the striking Badlands of North Dakota at Sully Springs on the afternoon of 29 June 1994. Powering the train is a EMD GP39E No. 2759, GE B30-7A No. 4049, EMD SW1200 No. 224 and a pair of GE C30-7s. The SW1200 switcher is traveling to Glendive, Montana, for some maintenance work.

A westbound Burlington Northern coal empty slinks through the Badlands past milepost 143 just west of Sully Springs, North Dakota, on the gorgeous early summer day of 29 June 1994.

An eastbound BN coal train snakes through the curves at Sully Springs, North Dakota, on 29 June 1994. The train is led by EMD SD60M No. 1991 that BN specially painted to honor U.S. troops serving in Operation Desert Storm in the Gulf War. A large seal of the United States graced the mostly white front of the locomotive. On the sides were large 11' x 6' oval logos that included words reading 'Pulling For Freedom' and 'Supporting Our Troops'.

A westbound Burlington Northern coal train crosses the Little Missouri River leaving the town of Medora, North Dakota, on 30 June 1994. Powering the train is BN EMD SD60M Nos 9243 and 9280.

Heading west over Montana Rail Link's Second Subdivision is BN train 123, approaching Louisville, Montana, after climbing Winston Hill on the afternoon of 2 July 1994.

Powered by a pair of EMD SD40-2s, Burlington Northern's Second 196 curves over Greenhorn Trestle while dropping downgrade on Mullan Pass between Skyline and Weed, Montana, on 3 July 1994.

The first section of BN train 120 has almost finished rounding the large horseshoe curve that crosses Greenhorn Creek between Skyline and Weed, Montana, on the morning of 3 July 1994.

Burlington Northern train 196 approaches the deep cut that was once a tunnel through Iron Ridge between Weed and Austin, Montana, as it descends the steep 2.2 per cent grade of Mullan Pass on 4 July 1994.

As a storm rumbles over Powder River Basin in the background, an eastbound Burlington Northern coal train led by GE C30-7 No. 5109 rolls through Donkey Creek Junction east of Gillette, Wyoming, on 6 July 1994. The train is leaving the Orin Line and heading east on the Black Hills Subdivision.

A BN coal train crawls through Wendover Canyon, just north (west) of Wendover, Wyoming, on 8 July 1994. Pulling the train is BN EMD SD40-2 No. 7198, with three GE C30-7s and another SD40-2 trailing.

Dropping downgrade through the horseshoe curve below Belmont on Nebraska's Crawford Hill is an empty Burlington Northern coal train headed for reloading in Powder River Basin. Three GE C30-7s and two EMD SD40-2s power the westbound train on a sunny 9 July 1994.

A rare treat among all of the coal trains, Burlington Northern EMD F9A-2 No. BN-1 crests the top of Crawford Hill at Belmont, Nebraska, on the point of an eastbound intermodal train on 9 July 1994. Behind BN-1 is F9B-2 No. BN-2 and two EMD SD40-2s, which are on the drawbar of five of BN's business cars up front in the train. Both of the F units were rebuilt in 1990, and are painted in new Grinstein colors.

A trio of new EMD SD70MAC locomotives that were built to haul coal grind upgrade as they approach the top of Crawford Hill at Belmont, Nebraska, on 9 July 1994.

On an eastbound Burlington Northern coal train clawing up Crawford Hill west of Belmont, Nebraska, on 9 July 1994, EMD SD70MAC Nos 9440 and 9449 bracket EMD SD60MAC No. 9503. EMD built four 3,800 hp SD60MAC as testbeds for A.C. traction and new HTCR trucks. This led to the development of the 4,000 hp A.C. traction SD70MAC that BN bought in large quantities. Nos 9440 and 9449 are only a couple of months old at this point, built in April and May 1994.

Two Oakway Leasing EMD SD60s, along with a pair of green associates, pull a coal train toward Belmont and the summit of Nebraska's Crawford Hill on 9 July 1994.

A westbound Burlington Northern empty coal train led by EMD SD60M No. 9226 approaches the town of Crawford, Nebraska, while on the south main a coal load storms out of town with four EMD SD40-2 helpers splicing a fuel tender screaming on the rear as the eastbound train hits the grade on 9 July 1994.

A westbound BN freight passes through Budd near East Dubuque, Illinois, on the afternoon of 21 August 1994. Cascade green EMD GP38-2 No. 2107 leads newer GP39-2 No. 2737, on a train that, in a photo, almost looks like a publicity shot with all of those matching BN auto racks.

On 17 September 1994, a BN local is about to depart Rochelle, Illinois. Leading the train is BN EMD GP9 No. 1977, a former Spokane, Portland & Seattle locomotive built by EMD in June of 1956, and set up to operate long hood forward.

Just after departing the taconite ore plant at Keewatin, a pair of Burlington Northern EMD SD60Ms head the train of steaming iron ore pellets westbound as it approaches the U. S. Highway 169 overpass just west of Keewatin, Minnesota, on 23 September 1994.

The brakeman from a BN local, powered by EMD SD9 No. 6150, is on the ground inspecting the passage of an ore train at Gunn, Minnesota, on 23 September 1994. When the train led by EMD SD60M No. 9287 clears the Sixth Subdivision junction switch at Gunn, the local will head to Kelly Lake.

An eastbound Burlington Northern local, powered by venerable EMD SD9 No. 6150, crosses a bridge near Holman, Minnesota, on 23 September 1994.

Burlington Northern train 34, powered by a pair of EMD GP50s, wheel eastward over the Rock River at Oregon, Illinois, on 22 October 1994.

In the Sand Hills of Nebraska, a Burlington Northern coal train is westbound on the spring day of 11 May 1995. BN EMD SD40-2 No. 7925 leads a pair of GE C30-7s dressed in BN and Santa Fe flavors on this coal empty west of Antioch.

A BN coal empty is westbound out of Ashby, Nebraska, destined for Alliance on a trip through the Sand Hills on 11 May 1995. A trio of EMD SD60s power the train – Oakway Leasing Nos 9053 and 9069 – along with a gray Kansas City Southern No. 724.

Three Burlington Northern SD70MACs on a northbound coal empty will soon meet a southbound Chicago & North Western load on the Orin Line main, while C&NW No. 8803 slowly moves forward while loading on the spur into Antelope Mine at Converse Junction, Wyoming, on 12 May 1995.

12,000 horsepower's worth of EMD SD70MAC locomotives scream by with a southbound coal train on the Orin Line south of Bill, Wyoming, on the morning of 12 May 1995. Burlington Northern SD70MACs were commonly called 'Grinsteins' after BN Chairman Gerald Grinstein, who was influential in the development of BN's final paint scheme.

Two Burlington Northern coal trains meet in a late snowfall on 13 May 1995, at Reno Junction … ah, springtime in Wyoming's Powder River Basin!

A BN local heads east into Oregon, Illinois, on the morning of 1 July 1995. Leaving the C&I (Chicago & Iowa) main line on the right is the 6.8-mile Mount Morris branch.

Burlington Northern train 143 marches westbound over the Wisconsin River Bridge near Prairie du Chain, Wisconsin, on the warm morning of 30 July 1995.

BN 'Expediter' intermodal train 42, on the right, speeds by local power at Rochelle, Illinois, on the afternoon of 12 August 1995. BN No. 1592 is a former Northern Pacific EMD GP18 (No. 377) that was remanufactured and modernised into a GP28P in March 1993.

Burlington Northern train 120 crosses Austin Creek Trestle just west of Skyline, Montana, as it descends Mullan Pass on 9 September 1995. The eastbound freight is powered by three EMD SD40-2s and a GE B30-7A cabless unit.

Low clouds hang over the Elkhorn Mountains as an eastbound BN grain train drops downgrade off Winston Hill, Montana, on 10 September 1995. Up front is EMD GP50 No. 3106 followed by two LMX GE B39-8s on this train utilising Montana Rail Link's Second Subdivision.

Beginning the arduous climb over Mullan Pass is Burlington Northern train 123 at Tobin, just west of Helena, Montana, on 10 September 1995. A portion of the city of Helena can be seen in the background.

BN train 120 follows the water's edge as it negotiates Lombard Canyon between Toston and Lombard, Montana, on the afternoon of 11 September 1995.

Passing through the semaphores at mile 219.8, Burlington Northern train 123 heads west escaping some stormy weather on Winston Hill, Montana, on 10 September 1995.

Burlington Northern grain train G02 climbs Winston Hill east of Louisville, Montana, passing through the semaphores at mile 224.7 on 12 September 1995.

On the afternoon of 28 December 1995, a BN local freight arrives at Rochelle, Illinois, as a 'caboose hop', which is defined as only a locomotive(s) and caboose operating as a train.

BN locomotives used on locals out of Rochelle, Illinois, rest on the night of 30 December 1995 during a light snowfall. BN EMD GP39E No. 2938 is a former Burlington GP35, while GP28M No. 1538 is a former Northern Pacific GP9. Both units were remanufactured by EMD and painted in the 'whiteface' scheme.

Burlington Northern EMD GP39E No. 2759 shows off its bold 'whiteface' colors at Rochelle, Illinois, on the afternoon of 10 April 1996.

A pair of vintage EMD SD9s power a BN welded rail train past the station at Rochelle, Illinois, on the afternoon of 10 April 1996.

A climb up a tall bluff at Trempealeau, Wisconsin, yields this view of the Mississippi River valley and Burlington Northern's long causeway just east of Winona, Minnesota. On the morning of 15 June 1996, a long BN 'Expediter' intermodal train 42 slices its way over the impressive route on the Wisconsin side of the river.

A Burlington Northern coal train powered by a matching quartet of GE C30-7s is ready to leave Alliance, Nebraska, on the eve of 4 July 1996. The city of Alliance gets hammered by a pretty good thunderstorm, courtesy of Mother Nature.

A westbound BN coal train smokes it up as it negotiates an undulating main line through West Berea, Nebraska, on 4 July 1996. This train is heading west on the Butte Subdivision, which crosses Crawford Hill on the way to the next crew change point of Edgemont, South Dakota.

A trio of EMD SD70MACs begin to pull as they depart Edgemont, South Dakota, with a loaded coal train on the afternoon of 5 July 1996. Afternoon clouds are building in the heat of the day, signaling a possibility of rain.

Three Burlington Northern EMD SD70MACs claw at the rails with a heavy coal train climbing Crawford Hill, east of Crawford, Nebraska, on 5 July 1996. Needless to say when looking at the photos on these two pages, Grinstein-painted SD70MAC locomotives were the king of the coal trains during this era.

A westbound BN coal empty crosses a small bridge west of Marietta, South Dakota, on the railroad's Black Hills Subdivision west of Edgemont on the afternoon of 5 July 1996.

A quartet of Cascade green EMD SD40-2s put all of their might into pushing a hefty coal train upgrade over Crawford Hill, east of Crawford, Nebraska, on 5 July 1996. To slake the locomotive's penchant for diesel is a unique fuel tender, which also provides more time between refueling stops.

A BN coal train curves along the North Platte River through scenic Wendover Canyon, Wyoming, on 6 July 1996. The lead BN GE C30-7 looks a bit different, with the usual blanked headlight receptacle missing from the nose, perhaps removed during a shop repair.

Remote Wendover Canyon is host to yet another BN coal train between Wendover and Cassa, Wyoming, on the afternoon of 6 July 1996.

A coal train climbs Crawford Hill, Nebraska, on 7 July 1996, and leading the train is an all-Cascade green consist of two EMD SD60Ms and two GE C30-7s. This gentle horseshoe curve is below the more famous one located just upgrade, and Sawlog Road can be seen following the tracks here.

A helper set consisting of a trio of Burlington Northern SD40-2s splicing a fuel tender push hard on a heavy eastbound coal train climbing Crawford Hill, east of Crawford, Nebraska, on 7 July 1996.

A heavy coal train is on its hands and knees as it works up Crawford Hill, west of Belmont, Nebraska, on 7 July 1996. Three BN EMD SD70MACs power the train and is getting some needed help from a pusher set of four Cascade green BN SD40-2s on the rear. The train is wrapped in the large horseshoe curve below Belmont, with the head end passing Breezy Point.

Four Burlington Northern GE C30-7s pull hard on a coal train rounding Breezy Point, west of Belmont, Nebraska, on the climb over Crawford Hill on 7 July 1996. In the background on the other side of the horseshoe curve is the end of the train and a helper set of three EMD SD40-2 locomotives and a fuel tender.

Burlington Northern's very unique Trough Train bends around a curve at Emerald, Nebraska, on 8 July 1996. These huge 278-foot, thirteen-unit articulated cars were designed by BN and built by Johnstown America Corporation. Each monster car had a stenciled capacity of 28,740 cubic feet. There were twenty-three cars built and this train could haul an equivalent of 146 standard coal hoppers, at a reduced weight due to lighter construction weight of these aluminum cars.

BN train 196 traces the Missouri River through Lombard Canyon as it approaches Lombard, Montana, on 9 August 1996. Three EMD locomotives power the eastbound train – a pair of SD40-2s and a GP50.

On the sunny afternoon of 10 August 1996, an eastbound BN intermodal train navigates the long bridge crossing a part of Lake Pend Oreille between Algoma and Sandpoint, Idaho.

Burlington Northern train 123 rolls smartly through Donlan, Montana, as it passes a semaphore at mile 208.6 on Montana Rail Link's Fourth Subdivision on 10 August 1996.

BN EMD GP50 No. 3131 leads train 125 westbound past the mile 207.2 semaphore on the MRL's former Northern Pacific main line between St. Regis and Paradise at Donlan, Montana, on 12 August 1996.

Eastbound train 52 approaches the west end of Havre Yard, Montana, on 6 October 1996. Three green Burlington Northern EMD SD40-2 locomotives, Nos 8089, 7877 and 7892, power the intermodal.

A westbound Burlington Northern intermodal train soars over the impressive bridge spanning Old Maids Coulee and Cut Bank Creek at Cut Bank, Montana, on 7 October 1996. Three BN EMD SD40-2s, along with a GE B30-7A, are joined by a leased Montana Rail Link, former Susquehanna EMD SD45, as power on the hotshot.

A quartet of Burlington Northern EMD SD40-2s and a cabless GE B30-7A B unit power westbound unit grain train G05 across Two Medicine Bridge at East Glacier, Montana. The Cascade green train stands out nicely among fall colours that have reached their peak on 8 October 1996.

Two BN EMD SD40-2 pusher locomotives give some help to westbound loaded grain train G05 as it crosses Two Medicine Bridge at East Glacier, Montana, on 8 October 1996.

A pair of Burlington Northern EMD SD40-2 helper locomotives push an eastbound freight and are entering Shed 7 between Java and Blacktail, Montana, on 9 October 1996. Helper locomotives working out of Essex provide help to both westbound and eastbound trains crossing the grades of Marias Pass.

Intermodal train 7, led by Burlington Northern SD40-2 No. 8075, exits Tunnel 3.9 and is about to enter Tunnel 4, east of Belton, Montana, on 9 October 1996. The train is running along the Middle Fork of the Flathead River on the scenic western portion of the Hi Line Subdivision route over Marias Pass that parallels on the southern border of Glacier National Park.

Two horses are more interested in the photographer than the passing eastbound intermodal train rumbling by, east of Bison, Montana, on the pretty autumn morning of 9 October 1996.

We end with a photo taken of the Burlington Northern when it was in the prime of its life. In September 1984, a caboose trails a northbound BN local freight past the towering bluffs along the Mississippi River at Trail of Tears State Park north of Cape Girardeau, Missouri, in old Frisco territory. As the caboose disappears around the next curve, I hope you have enjoyed this look at BN in its final years.